Of Living
Thinking and Being

Written by Paul Francis Griffiths
Illustrated by Aidan Roberts

Of Living, Thinking and Being
Copyright © 2022 by Paul Francis Griffiths

All rights reserved. No part of this publication may be reproduced, distributed, or transmitted in any form or by any means, including photocopying, recording, or other electronic or mechanical methods, without the prior written permission of the author, except in the case of brief quotations embodied in critical reviews and certain other non-commercial uses permitted by copyright law.

Tellwell Talent
www.tellwell.ca

ISBN
978-0-2288-5472-2 (Paperback)

The deep rest of regular nightly sleep
 is a fundamental of living well.

Make quality of sleep a priority,
or you may fail in the simplest tasks.

However, do not be undisciplined;
sleep only when it is time to sleep well.

**Do not rush from your bed in the morning;
give yourself time to awaken fully.**

**Prepare your mind for the oncoming day,
feet to floor with certainty of purpose.**

**Make your bed the day's first accomplishment;
a tidy space leaves room for getting up.**

**Above all else, your health is paramount,
and essential for a quality life.**

**Your body is the vehicle of your journey;
your mind is the guide for the path.**

**Your spirit is the force driving you forward;
heed every aspect of wellbeing.**

Regular exercise heralds' verdure,
a daily morning routine is vital.

Make your body as strong as it may be,
it is an asset to be highly prized.

Time spent improving your physical health;
is time that may be considered well spent.

Counter point to the body is the mind,
meditations are most beneficial.

Serene stillness devoid of conscious thought,
enables the mind to reset itself.

Clarity of thought is achieved this way,
bringing the path ahead into focus.

By preparing both your mind and body,
insurmountable willpower can grow.

Inner fortitude comes forth as needed,
from a wellspring that surges within you.

Critical to unlocking potential
is the attainment of self-mastery.

Break your fast with regularity,
make refuelling your body a habit.

Let unhurried simplicity guide you,
wisely choosing nourishment and pleasure.

Do not succumb to gluttonous desire,
too much of a good thing is still too much.

Prioritise your daily ablutions,
let no slip mar the features of your face.

Be deliberate in choosing attire,
external appearance resounds intent.

Stay focused while cleansing and closeted,
present yourself to the world with purpose.

Make yourself a careful student of life,
observe well and learn from other's errors.

Find a hand hold in what is well researched,
tested and so proven reliable.

A solid grounding gives stability,
much surer than the footing of a fool.

**Apply yourself well to your vocation,
and also to pursuits of interest.**

**Strive for excellence in your enterprise,
own your success but do not be boastful.**

**View failures as a mark of your progress,
stand tall knowing you have given your all.**

**Be wise, retain the rewards of labour,
fiscal responsibility seeds wealth.**

**Wait not for windfall; you must shake the tree,
glean what you may, make of it what you can.**

**Plan for the future, it pays dividends;
regularity will compound your growth.**

**Let competition inspire excellence,
strive to achieve a true greatness of self.**

**Seek your victory with integrity,
do not win at the expense of the game.**

**Your opponents are your greatest ally
because of the challenges they provide.**

Kindness to strangers is a worthy trait,
especially to those who are in need.

A smile and a friendly word cost you naught,
but the return is often substantial.

Charity serves both those who give and who receive,
be open to being either.

You should choose your friends with the utmost caution;
they will inform your path throughout life.

As currents affect the course of a boat,
so too a friend's influence can be felt.

Undesirable habits may emerge if you strive
to impress the unworthy.

Greatly value the boon of true friendship;
it is worth providing and receiving.

Friends will rejoice in each other's success,
sharing triumphs, life's blessings thus doubled.

Friends also make life's burdens more bearable,
supporting each other in hardship.

Cultivate fortitude and integrity,
prudence, equanimity, and tact.

Embody those traits you seek in others;
be the companion you anticipate.

Remain resolute in your convictions,
like-minded people will be drawn together.

Be mindful of thoughts you dwell upon;
they can greatly influence your wellbeing.

Have gratitude for the things you possess,
it will serve you better than self-pity.

Do not dwell on darkness, examine ideas in the light,
seek the help you need.

It is human to seek your hearts desires,
but it's wise to first seek to know yourself.

Strive to achieve those things of which you dream,
steer yourself toward them confidently.

Still, hold them loose, for life is capricious,
goals and ideals may change over time.

**Reflect every evening on your day's work;
be pleased with yourself and your achievements.**

**Acknowledge your emotions and
feel them so they do not weigh you down later on.**

**Keep your goals for tomorrow in your mind,
focus on your plans and likely prospects.**

**The deep rest of regular nightly sleep
is a fundamental of living well.**

**Make quality of sleep a priority,
or you may fail in the simplest tasks.**

**However, do not be undisciplined,
sleep only when it is time to sleep well... and that time is now, Goodnight.**

www.ingramcontent.com/pod-product-compliance
Lightning Source LLC
LaVergne TN
LVHW071732060526
838200LV00031B/479